On the Assembly Line

Folklore from the Factory Floor

By Fred McTaggart

On the Assembly Line
Copyright, 1968, 2018
Fred McTaggart
Written for a course in American Folk Literature
University of Iowa
May 7, 1968

FOREWORD

The labor lore presented here was compiled for a folklore class, taught by the late Harry Oster, at the University of Iowa in 1968. I transcribed the anecdotes and stories from interviews I conducted with UAW workers and retirees who had spent much of their working lives in automobile and agricultural implement plants, mostly during the 1930s and 1960s. My commentary is based to a large degree on my own experiences working as a community/membership relations representative for the UAW from 1964 to 1967.

On the Assembly Line was not published at the time but was later part of a collection of Professor Oster's materials donated to the Iowa State Archives. I am publishing it now and selling it for a minimal price with the hope that it might be a valuable resource for folklorists, labor historians, students, and unionists.

Since first attempts to organize workers on an industry-wide basis–by Eugene Debs, the "Wobblies," and later the CIO–the factory worker has been bombarded with material which is intended to be passed along through folk channels. During major strikes or organizing battles, workers have been taught protest songs written by Joe Hill, Ralph Chaplin, or Woody Guthrie; and union convention halls still ring with the militant strains of "Solidarity Forever." Thousands of slogans, rhymes, catch-words have been coined to express in memorable ways the workers' hatred of oppression and wage slavery. The early battles of labor–from the Cordwainers' strike up through the Pullman strike and the auto workers' sitdowns–are taught in labor education classes to give workers a sense of pride in their background and traditions.

Valuable as this material is, much of it has failed to germinate as folklore. Unless they have been through union education classes, most young workers today know little about the sitdown strikes or the battle of the overpass; they are often among the first to criticize the tactics of the late Martin Luther King, Jr. or of the student activists at Columbia University–tactics almost identical to those used in pioneer labor organization. Although union members learn and sing songs such as "Solidarity Forever," "We're Gonna Roll," and "We Shall Not Be Moved," at union schools and conventions, few of them are able to quote the words of any of these songs. Some of the strike slogans have survived, but in general, the material handed down from the 1930s does not circulate freely among workers in industrial unions.

Outside the shop, industrial workers like to think of themselves as "middle class" and they are often more interested in their status in suburbia than in their "class consciousness" as workers. However, inside the shop, the nature of the factory system, especially the assembly line, tends to isolate and alienate the worker from the rest of society, forcing him to look for support from the people with whom he works. In this situation, the union can provide the unifying structure, continuity, and stability needed to channel the workers' fears, desires, and frustrations into traditional patterns. In this sense, workers are constantly creating a folklore of their own–one that is separate from but not opposed to that handed down by the Wobblies and CIO organizers. This lore is

centered on the hardships and trials of the assembly line and the focus is not on the union heroes of the past or the labor leaders of today but rather the local union stewards and committeemen–the representatives who have day-to-day contact with the worker on the job.

For this paper, I have drawn on material given me in four interviews with members of the UAW International Union plus personal experience gained through three years of work in public relations and education for the UAW, during which time I came in contact with union members from eight states in the Middle and South West. Of those interviewed, two are retirees–Clyde Keown of St. Louis Local 25 (Chevrolet-Fisher Body) and Mike Cole of Des Moines, Iowa Local 991 (Ford Implement). Ed Coffey, a veteran of early organizing battles of Kansas City Local 93

(Chevrolet), is Education Director for Region 5 of the UAW; and Jack Bishop of Des Moines Local 991 is a young local union officer who has accumulated all of his work experience since the Korean War. Thus two of the informants come from massive auto assembly plants; two come from a smaller agricultural implement operations in a rural area. Two are now retired; the other two are still active in union work. As a representative of the younger workers, Jack Bishop provides some interesting insights into the changing nature of union-management relations.

While there is a wide difference in the backgrounds of the four informants, I found little difference in the type of material transmitted. Although all four have been or are presently in some position of responsibility with the union and hence should be expected to be familiar with the songs, legends, and slogans passed down from the 1930s, the material which they chose to record emphasizes not the battles of labor history but the conditions of the assembly line. The bulk of the material is in the form of anecdotes, nearly all of them culled from personal experience but often told in striking detail and with a great deal of implicit commentary on conditions in the shop. As they are told in narrative fashion, the stories often closely resemble the style of folk tales and hero legends, even though the narrators insist that they witnessed the events first-hand. In some cases, it would seem to me that the narrators unconsciously exaggerated or altered their experiences into folk patterns. At any rate, the fact that these events are remembered and recorded while thousands of others are forgotten provides insight into what seems important to the narrator and which events he is likely to pass on to future workers. In addition to the anecdotes, I also found customs, practical jokes, rumors, terminology or dialect, slogans, and legends–all of which provide insights into the hopes, aspirations, and fears of industrial workers. Each item reflects in some way on how the assembly line affects the lives of workers and their associations as union members.

Anecdotes, Jokes, Customs

Running through all the material is the hardship of life on the assembly line–whether it is during the back-breaking days of the 1930s or the more affluent present. As it is seen through the eyes of Ed Coffey, conditions at the Chevrolet plant in Kansas City, Missouri during the middle '30s became nearly unbearable without the union:

I remember, for example, on the line putting on radiators, I come in that morning at six o'clock, went to work at 7 o'clock, and quit at noon–a half hour for lunch–back at 12:30 and at 6 o'clock that night, while I was tightening a radiator with a 220 high cycle, haunched down in front of the thing, walking backwards, worn out, couldn't hardly straighten up any more, I saw the familiar feet go by, as the superintendent of the line. And I said, 'Mr. Fox, when are we going home?' And without breaking his stride, out of the side of his mouth, he says, 'When the god damn whistle blows!' Well, it's this kind of thing that brought the union about–largely because of the inhuman treatment of 12 hours on the job, no idea of when they're going to quit, hungry, and tired. But you had to hold on to that job.

In contrast, Jack Bishop, vice president of UAW Local 991 in Des Moines, has never directly experienced these conditions of long hours and low pay. He has worked at Ford Implement since 1955–a period when union benefits are reportedly at their highest peak in history, and he works under a contract that is supposed to be one of the best in the country–the Ford national agreement. Yet his commentary on life on the assembly line differs from Coffey's only in degree and intensity:

It's very hard to explain an assembly line to someone who has never worked on one. It's a very boring type job, of course; and there was an article wrote once by a guy that said when you work on an assembly line, the best thing to do is leave your brains at home. And I think this pretty well describes it because you learn a routine and

*then you continue this all day long, except for
your relief time and your noon lunch break.*

Whether in the 1930s or 1960s, the assembly line, with its constant repetitive grind, is the common enemy of all, and the workers react with frustration, anger, bitterness, violence, or good humor–depending on the time and circumstances. Always the assembly line moves on, and it is up to the worker to keep up with the pace of production.

Clyde Keown, 77, a retiree of Chevrolet Local 25 in St. Louis, said:

They give you an area to work in and if you don't have time to do that job in that length of space, then there's too much on that job. If you don't quit when you hit that spot, then the other guy is supposed to come on and do his job and you can't run him in the hole. You'd have the whole thing upset then. You have to stay in that space you have to work in and you aren't supposed to go in the hole.

Line speed and time allotted for each job is a constant problem and workers have struggled for years in order to get some control over line speed. As Ed Coffey puts it:

Well, there was a rheostat on the line, and if they had a little stoppage or if they got behind on their average hourly production, why any supervisor could walk up and turn that rheostat, and you could

The control of workers over production speed is still negligible, and nearly every year auto workers take strike votes concerning "production standards"–a euphemism for assembly line speed. Less than 10 years ago, the Des Moines local waged the longest strike of its history because two welders (experienced men with good work records, according to Jack Bishop and Mike Cole) were fired when they could not keep up with the work standard set for their job. The workers banded together with determination until the workers were taken back and the work standard changed. As Jack Bishop put it, "The people were quite disturbed about that because they (the men fired) were both long-time employees with good work, labor relations records and they (the workers) realized that if they could fire these kind of people for not making a certain amount of production, then certainly that they would be the next."

In this case, the workers reacted with determination to what they considered a grave situation. In many cases, however, the reaction is more light-hearted as in this "initiation procedure" for the new worker on the assembly line at Des Moines:

I'll Get It (Jack Bishop)

If a guy's having a little trouble, the guy below him will say, 'let it go and I'll get it,' and, of course, he lets it go, but he doesn't get it; he just goes on by, you know. And they'll do this to a new guy on the line a lot. Pretty soon, the foreman comes up and asks him how come he's not getting his parts on, you know. And he will say, 'Well that guy said...'

Normally, the guy's already got so much work to do, he couldn't catch it if he wanted to, you know. They keep you pretty busy anyhow.

The worker soon learns that the line is no joke, but he can get along if he maintains his sense of humor. Viewed from the right perspective, the obstacle course of mechanical operations can provide some slapstick humor–for the man who is not the victim.

The Body Wrench (Ed Coffey)

hey always seemed to put the tall man on a short man's job and a short man on a tall man's job, like in the pit, they put...I worked in the pit (he stands about 6 foot 3), and I was always bumping my head on cotter pins or sharp corners (he laughs). For example, you got so used to a certain clearance in the pit sometimes that a large sheet of cardboard they put on the floor of the pit to catch the paint and stuff–they would take that out every night and put in fresh and sometimes they would get behind and wouldn't take the old out, and the next morning, we would come in there, and we would always bump our heads, if we were tall enough. We were allowing just enough that that one thickness of cardboard made the difference between bumping your head and not bumping your head. But they put one guy on the job that seemed to fit. He was of medium height, barrel chested, quite heavy–not fat, but he was just a heavy guy. And they put him on the body bolt wrench. This was a 220 high cycle. You hold a ring with one hand, and you've got an arm that goes back under your arm pit, and then you operate the shank which is on the clutch and a universal joint on the end. And they showed him how to operate this wrench, and he did all right except that one time that the arm underneath his arm pit got away from him and swung out on the other side, and that clutch took hold and started chattering on that bolt up there and down in the pit like that. You have your wrench outlet in the wall and cords are all over the place and unless you knew, the quickest way to find that cord outlet was to take the cord and follow it to the wall. And this wrench was beating this guy something awful. Just bang, bang, bang against his chest (laugh) bang, bang, bang, bang (beats his own chest while imitating the sound) real hard, and he just slid right down the wall and set on the floor, and we finally found where his wrench was hooked up and pulled it out of the wall, and then when it stopped, he says, 'Why didn't you shut it off sooner?' He was through; he got up and crawled out of that pit, and there must have been 15 jobs go down the line with all the body bolts loose because, you know, of this one incident. Makes a lot of difference.

In contrast to the slapstick comedy of this anecdote, there is often a great deal of pathos in stories told about workers who could not keep up with the jobs assigned them. There is a certain heroic quality reminiscent of John Henry in two of these characters: the tappet adjustor who did the work of three men and the big fellow who burned out his machine keeping up with the time standard placed on his job.

The Man Who Didn't Hurry (Ed Coffey)
Yeah, I know of people who literally drove themselves into a sick person just trying to keep up, and I know of one wonderful fat old man–not old man, he was a young man, but he was fat but he had very quick hands. For example, he adjusted all the tappets on a six-cylinder car doing 40 jobs an hour plus other work. Just adjusting the tappets, that wasn't all–he did other work. And they decided to give him some

more because he wasn't running like others were–hurrying to keep up. He would move from one job to another, and every motion he made counted, and he was a wonderful guy. And they gave him more work to do, and he wouldn't take it, and they fired him. They literally fired that man. And they had to keep three people on his job to keep it up,...for the first week or 10 days; then they got it down, moved it down to two people, but they never did get down to one man to do the job. Never.

In the next story, narrated by Mike Cole, the man, in tall tale tradition, comes out victorious not only over the machine but also over the hated foreman and time study man, as well.

The Rate Was Too High (Mike Cole)

Well, the best story that I ever heard of, of a fellow that was fast. We had a fellow who stood about 6 foot 2, and he was a real speed demon. I mean he was a real–he was a good worker wherever you put him. He was in the press room, and he was on a big press. And they time studied the job, and they set the rate way out of this world. I think it was 700 and some an hour–pieces to run off. And this big fellow and the time study man and the foreman come along and jumped on him 'cause he wasn't making the rate. He said, 'but it can't be done on this machine, and I've told you it couldn't.' And they said, 'well, you make it. We might just take a notion to fire you if you don't make it.' 'Now you guys just stand there and watch me.' And that foreman stood there...and that time study guy. And that guy was running that machine so fast and feeding pieces through it that the machine got so hot that the press wouldn't run. And he'd wait until it'd cool off, and he'd go right after it again, and finally the foreman said to the time study man, 'Buddy, you'd better get a new rate set on here because that guy's gonna tear this machine up here for you.' He said, 'He's running it now so fast that it just isn't going to stand it.' So by golly just about then the old machine clunked, and the motor burned out on her.

These stories both illustrate perfectly the psychology of mass production and the need for unity in the face of its impersonal grind. The workers who become heroes are not just speedy and dexterous. They are unpretentious men whose ability on the job is exploited by the common enemies–the assembly line, the foreman, and the time study man. But if given a fair chance, they can, like Mike Cole's "speed demon," defeat all three.

In direct contrast are the men who are fast but who try to beat the system at the expense of their fellow workers. To Ed Coffey, they are "job killers"; to Mike Cole, they are "bright-haired boys." In each case, the men are scorned because, while gaining favor for themselves, they make life harder for other workers on the line. As Coffey explained:

We were pretty mean at times, even to our own people, especially some guy that we didn't like because of his–if he intended to kill a job, you know, or not really do a decent thing towards a job. A fellow that would come in in the morning a half hour before the line started and work solidly that whole half hour doing bench work in preparation for the rest of the day. And then during the work hours, why he would have an opportunity to goof off by eating a sandwich or something like this or laughing at the rest of the guys. And then oftentimes, these fellows, when they were doing this work in the morning and having this time on their hand, sometimes a foreman would come by and give them more work to do, and they'd do it. And then the next guy that would come along to do that job, why he'd have to do it, like on the second shift. He'd have to take the whole job assignment. So we tended to call these guys job-killers.

And in much the same way, Mike Cole draws a clear distinction between the really fast workers and the company's "speed demons" who set job rates which were unrealistic for other workers.

But we've had guys, we've had welders who have just been borned (sic) with speed and a lot of time the company will take those fellows and maybe find a couple of them and put them on welding fixture jobs that, for goodness sake, they could make a rate that an ordinary person couldn't even dream of. These are 'bright-haired boys'–that's what we'd call them. They're the company pets; the company will take them and put them on this job and say, 'Now, really whoop it up here for me.' And then they really set the rate up. Well, then they take two other guys and put them on the job and the guys say, 'I can't make that rate.' And they say, 'Well, Bob and Joe over there, they made it for us.' And the guys will say, 'I can't help it; I can't make it.' And they say, 'Well, we're going to give you three days off without pay.' And, well then, of course, the boys, they'd ask for their committeeman.

But the funniest part of it is once they had one of these set, they take these guys over then and put them on a real good job. They could goof off maybe four hours out of the eight and then just take it easy and loaf along, you see, and they'd have a real good rate to work by.

Thus, the over-zealous worker, whether he is naturally speedy or whether he comes in early to set up his stock, creates a problem for other workers on the assembly line–a problem that is reflected in practical jokes, such as the following, related by Ed Coffey:

Four in the Mouth and One in the Wrench
(Ed Coffey)

Well, Herb Buick worked clear up at the end of the pit, and there was a large pipe that went across the pit behind him, and they built a counter-like thing, and a fellow name of Stinky Davis, worked with his stock off of that counter. And behind him was Hugh Wilson, who was working the step-hanger wrench. And this fellow Davis, uh Stinky Davis, would go to every job with four bolts–5/16 hex-head bolts with anti-squeak flat washer and lock washer on each one. So that he kept his job always ahead by making up the stock–the bolt, the flat washer and the anti-squeak and the lock washer. He would have this made up–a whole series of pans, these one-loaf bread pans stacked up on this counter. And he would go to the job with four of those bolts in his mouth plus one in the wrench and one in the hand with his grip pin and an air wrench. And his job was to put those front fender to body bolts in. Reach way up high on the side and be gone until he put all six of them in and tighten them up. And it was quite a mean job. So one day, Herb Buick took a half an orange, and he squeezed this orange juice all over the stock, and Hugh Wilson saw him do it. In fact, I think they had it made up before, so Stinky went back and loaded up again and went to his job and Hugh

Wilson stood up behind him and said, 'Hey Stinky, do you know what that damn Buick done?' 'Uh, no.' 'He peed in your stock.' (laugh) Well, uh, he had the orange stuff in his mouth and spewed them out on the floor in between the running board and the aisle of the surface and dropped his air wrench and went back to the counter, and he took every one of those bread pans and threw them out on the floor–just threw them. He had all his stock made up, but he just threw them out. And, wouldn't you know, Cantrell, or what was his name?...the plant superintendent went hurrying up the...and this plant superintendent was always half running when he walked, and he always had his nose stuck up in the air (laugh), and he didn't see those bolts. (laugh) He took about two steps into those bolts and fell flat on his back–right on top of the bolts. We had a hell of a time keeping that guy's job. (laugh) This was before the union.

While the attitude here is light-hearted, there is poetic justice not only for the man who so carefully prepared his stock ahead of time but also for the plant superintendent who hurries through the plant with his nose stuck up in the air. Although the workers here do not seem to act in anger (and they do try to save Stinky's job for him), the matter of speed-ups on the assembly line is a serious business, and the workers have no sympathy for men who make matters worse for everyone.

Among the most hated enemies in this regard is the time-study man or "efficiency expert" who comes in from the outside and tries to find the time standard that will give the company the greatest possible production schedule. As Ed Coffey points out, "Any intelligent person will find short cuts on the work that he does–not to fail to do the job but to find a way that you can do it quicker. But you don't let the supervisor find out about it." Because of this, "snooping" by supervisors and time study men often becomes an important issue in contract negotiations. The time study man who lurks behind the nearest pillar is a deadly enemy because once the time standard is set, once all the short-cuts have been discovered by management, then the worker has no relief from the grueling pace of the line. Coffey points out that time study men usually take their average in the morning when the worker is fresh and do not take into account the fatigue that slows down operations later in the day. The whole time-study process is "about 90 percent opinion," he adds.

Working hundreds of miles away in an agricultural implement plant, Mike Cole has many of the same sentiments: "I always say the only place you should use a stop watch is on a horse race–it shouldn't be used on the human race," he said. "I believe in a fair day's work for a fair day's pay, but I don't believe in giving the Ford Motor Company 12 hours of work for eight hours of pay." As seen in the following anecdote, the attitude of workers toward the time study man is often not so rational or good natured; but the results can be funny.

The Efficiency Expert (Mike Cole)

One time they had an efficiency expert come in the plant, and his name was Carrington, and he was a character, and he was going to make a complete time study–back when old Wood Brothers owned it. They was going to make a complete time study. And we had a night superintendent, his name was Clarence Walker. And the boys down on the assembly line during the day immediately made them a dummy, and the line wasn't running at night, and they put this guy's name on its chest, and they hung it from a rafter down on the assembly line. And Walker would always make a tour of the plant at night, and this was a darkened area down in there, just real pale-like. So he was going up the assembly line and saw this guy hanging there, and he thought somebody had committed suicide and

While the story has the mystery of a ghost tale in the ironic situation of the night superintendent, the significance probably lies in the attitude shown by the workers toward Carrington, the time-study man. While the story itself may be funny, hanging a man in effigy has a more serious connotation.

A matter equally as serious as line speed and time standards is the need of workers for relief time–time to get away from the job and take a smoke, get a drink of water or go to the rest room. With the constant movement of the assembly line, this is, of course, impossible except during the regular break periods–which until recently were only 15 minutes in the morning and 15 minutes in the afternoon in most auto plants. When the call of nature interferes with the call of the assembly line, a rather difficult situation emerges, as seen in the following anecdotes:

The Straw Hat (Ed Coffey)

We used to have a hell of a time getting any relief. You would train yourself to go all morning without going–for relief–any personal time at all. And once in awhile, you had a problem. And we had a guy by the name of Archie, he wore his summer hat in the fall–a sailor straw. And he was putting in the two-boards in this old Chevrolet, the old model Chevrolet, when they had the wooden two-boards, and he had a line job with stuff in his mouth–but that didn't have anything to do with this. He had to go, and he couldn't get no relief. (laugh) So he proceeded to just drop his work and drop his pants and unload in that straw hat (laugh) and he set it on that line. The line is a belt, you know, this surface. He just set it on the line. And it went on down the line. Of course, they identified the hat (laugh) and he was gone. They fired that poor guy, and all he had to do was just natural relief. Couldn't wait. So he did the next best thing he could think of. And they fired him.

The Five-Gallon Can (Jack Bishop)

Just a year ago, there was a guy working in the press room, and the foreman told him he was spending too much time in the rest room. So he got him a five gallon bucket and set it down by his machine there, and a little while later, he just went right ahead and used the five gallon bucket there by the machine, you know, and, of course, the foreman in this case didn't get mad about it or anything. He thought it was humorous, you know, and it was. But

The importance of relief time has not changed, even though almost 30 years have passed between the two incidents. However, the two incidents do reflect a changing trend in attitudes between the worker and the boss. An incident that was cause for discharge of a worker in the '30s becomes a practical joke that is accepted as such by the foreman in the 1960s.

While there is still a great deal of antagonism between workers and their supervisors, there now seems to be a clear understanding between them. With his job protected against arbitrary dismissal by the grievance procedure of the union, the worker has ways of dealing with the foreman who tries to abuse his position of power. As Jack Bishop puts it:

We've got some real militant guys on the line; if the foreman is giving them a bad time, and parts aren't fitting, they just let 'em go right on down and, of course, they have to shut the line down in order for them to get straightened out. And there's guys that if a foreman's been treating him bad, he turns around and treats the foreman the same way, in regards to if he's having trouble or if he's out of parts, he don't tell the foreman. He just stands there, you know, and waits for him to come around. He will say, 'Why didn't you tell me?' And he says, "I can't handle the whole plant, you know. If I'm going to work on this bench, then somebody's going to have to bring the parts to me, and if you want me to go get parts when I run out, then I'll go look for them, which could be at the other end of the plant, you know.' And the foreman understands this pretty well and knows if I'm going to get along with this guy, I'm going to have to treat him right, you know. He's in a position where he can cost me too. They understand this kind of thing. If you cut production by not cooperating to the fullest extent, well they understand this. It only hurts them....

Your more militant members are this way, and your ones that are more timid, they won't argue with the foreman; they'll just tell the foreman they want to see the committman. And, of course, the committeeman has to tell the foreman. 'If you're going to treat this guy this way, then this is the way your people are going to treat you.' And most of them (grievances) can be worked out right on the floor...because if a foreman's still bull-headed to the committeeman, he can go to the general foreman and tell him he's got a foreman that's crossways with some of his workers down there and he'd better get him straightened out if he wants to get any production out of them. And the general foreman will shape him up if what he's telling him is true.

While such a working relationship between worker and foreman seems only logical and reasonable, the struggle to reach such an understanding has been long, bitter and often violent. Being the middle man in the struggle between the union and the company, the foreman was often the one to suffer. As explained by Ed Coffey:

Oh, we had all kinds of ways of showing our extreme dislike for certain foremen. Of course, in the early days of the union, before we started operating so legally and with such finesse, an able bargaining committeeman would quickly decoy his supervisor over in the corner some place, where there was nobody but he and his supervisor, and he would rack up the supervisor real good, and, after giving him a hard time physically, pushed him around and shoved him around and striking him, why the supervisor would threaten to take this guy up to the front office for....And the committeeman would advise him: 'Well, it's your word against mine, and if you want to go ahead, you go ahead.' Or there were other times when things become so hot on the job between the union spokesman and the management guy that they would pick up a tool and run him back under a stock pile some place where they couldn't get at him. He'd hide or escape by getting away so they couldn't get at him physically. But nowadays, we operate with extreme finesse (laugh), we can't even...you have to watch how you hold your face when you say certain phrases. I guess you could call a foreman a bastard today, but you'd better be smiling when you say it in a friendly kind of way. If you say it in a point of anger, why you'd be subject to disciplinary layoff, which is frequently being done today.

Likewise, Clyde Keown tells about his foreman:

Then we had some foreman, fellow name of Smith, in the trim department, and he was very much against the people organizing the union and very much a company man. So the boys proceeded to take care of him. So one time we walked into a bar over there in front of the plant, and he was in there with some of the other foremen. We walked in on the man, and he run. He was scared to death. That was the way it was–they did things in the plant that they knew they shouldn't do, then when they got outside, they had no protection.

While experiences between workers and the boss were often violent, the anecdotes which have been passed down have a light, good-natured tone–a tone that is undoubtedly made possible by the fact that such violence is no longer necessary. In the following anecdote, Ed Coffey tells how his co-workers used a catch-word, derived from a joke which circulated among them, to describe the hated foreman.

Tally Ho (Ed Coffey)

I like the story that they used to tell about...it happened to be a Texan, who went to England, and he went to a fox hunt, and they decked him out with all of his regalia, and they gave him a horse, and the fox took off, and the hounds took off, and the riders took off, and they circled back, and pretty soon the Texan, he said, 'There goes the little son-of-a-bitch.' And the Englishman called him off to one side and said, 'We admire your, uh, quaint Texas language, but over here whenever you sight the fox, we always say, 'Tally ho.' So that became a saying down through the plant, that when a certain supervisor who was ruled obnoxious come walking by, why somebody would say, 'Tally ho!' and everybody on the line knew what they were talking about.

Aimed at the owner rather than the foreman, the next story, handed down among workers in the Des Moines plant and narrated by Jack Bishop shows the attitude of workers toward the "sob stories" handed down by management during collective bargaining or strike situations. Bishop heard the story from an older worker, now dead, who told it as a humorous story.

Please Save My Plant! (Jack Bishop)

I wasn't here at the time, but I understand that the guy who owned the plant before Ford had it. One time they was on strike, and a lot of the people were standing out in the street in front of the plant, and the guy come out, and he was begging with the people to come back, that they was going to break him, and they were going to break the plant, and they wouldn't have jobs. And he got down on his hands and knees, and he was begging. And then I guess he went into a prayer to save this plant, you know. And, I don't know, I think they was asking for a nickel raise or something. I don't recall how the story went, whether they got the raise or didn't, but the plant survived.

And a sideline on the same Mr. Woods, the former owner of the plant, is told by Mike Cole:

Santa Claus (Mike Cole)
Another story they used to tell on him, was at Christmas time, he come out and give everybody a peck of wormy apples.

In all of these anecdotes about bosses, there is an indirect definition of the "ideal" boss–the boss who is everything that the real bosses are not. Perhaps this "ideal boss" comes to life in the story told by Mike Cole from his short experience as the owner of a small coal mine. The attitude that a worker always has in mind the welfare of other workers–even should he be temporarily placed in the position of boss–is perhaps a typical one. Unlike Cole, most workers do not have the opportunity to show how they would behave as a boss.

The Boss Who Wouldn't Steal (Mike Cole)
Then I took a little fling in the coal mine. The water took it over. But the union, that was the thing–it wasn't the UAW at that time, it was the

old UMWA, the United Mine Workers. I had this little mine that I'd bought, and I had 22 people working for me, and they was all good union men. And I was the company. So I told them to elect a check weigh man. You see, at that time, with all the coal that come out of the mine, a lot of guys would have a check weigh man to mark down how much coal has come out of this mine for each miner so the company couldn't cheat him out of it. So we was setting in the–I had an old Studebaker engine that was a hoist to bring the cage to the coaler (?). So I was setting there figuring up the night's receipts, and the guys was standing around the stove; they had just come up. They had elected the check weigh man, and I called him over. I said, 'Come over here.' And he come over there, and I said, 'How come your figures don't tally with mine?' And he said, 'What do you mean?' And I said, 'You can see what I mean." And he said, 'Why I've been helping you; I've been taking 75 to 100 pounds of coal off of every car that come up here for you.

And I was just a little guy, and I reached over and took a pick handle and took a swipe at him and hit him across the shoulders, and he run out the door and run out along the creek and through the brush. And I said, 'What's the matter with you?'

They called me Beans, that was my nickname. They said, 'What's the matter with you, Beans?' And I said, 'Well, I just chased your check weigh man off.' 'What's the matter?' And I said, 'You guys figure it out. He's took anywhere from five pounds of coal to 100 pounds of coal off of every car that come up from that shaft today–he stole it off of you. Now the only thing I can do, because I don't know which ones he got it off of, I'm going to take the total here, and I'm going to divide it equal among every one of you that worked in that mine today, and I'll have it on your paycheck.' But, I said, 'if he ever comes back around here, I don't care if he's one of your union men or not, if he ever comes back here, I'm going to run him off with this pick handle again, because he ain't even going to work here as a coal miner. And they says, 'If he ever come back here, we'll drown him in the sulphur.'

The story tells not only the ideal qualifications for a boss, but also the qualities least admirable in a union man. In other words, here, we have a complete reversal of the usual worker-boss relationship–told from the point of view of a man who served at different times as both worker and boss.

Unfortunately, bosses like Mike Cole are not common in mass production industries; and in the early days of union organization, an antagonistic management could make things rough on those individuals who helped organize the union. Sometimes the action was indirect–by showing favoritism to those workers who opposed the union or who "buttered up" management. "The companies oftentimes had a special list they called the D list," said Ed Coffey, "where you would be called in to work extra if you were frequently found bringing a basket of tomatoes in off your garden to your supervisor or if you were available to do some work on the weekend or days off around the foreman's house–like painting or mowing the yard, or...these people found favors–extra work, extra income, more possibility of a guarantee of work when work was available–as opposed to the guys that stood off." At other times, discrimination against the union member would be much more direct and obvious, as in Coffey's experience with his trick knee:

I slipped my knee out once, and I went to a doctor, and the doctor put me in the St. Joseph Hospital. And they proceeded to decide they were going to have to operate, and, before I knew it, they had a cast on my leg, from my hip on down. And the next day, I went down to the plant to see if they could have a job for me to do. You know some of these company sucks, they would have a place where they would separate and mix stock, just set down and do it; but being a union guy, why if they couldn't find a job for me, I just had to go home. Except they finally figured out that I could paint the brightness on the bolts on the Army trucks, which meant that I would take my cast and this paint bucket and brush and walk down about three blocks to this backyard with water holes here and there and crawl back on toward there with my cast on and try to paint those nuts. And they expected me to turn it down, but when you refuse work, a job assignment, then you're subject to discharge. So I said, 'Well, okay, but meanwhile get my committeeman.' And they brought the committeeman on down, and I still hadn't got to the back door, I was walking so slow. But I hadn't refused to do the work. And the committeeman argued about it, but they wouldn't change their mind. I could either do that or go home. So I had to go home.

So I went home and cut that cast off and went to an osteopath, and he put my leg back in shape. (laugh) And I went back to work the next day on my regular job. But there was this kind of...you had these double standards going all the time.

Today, with stronger contract language that has been negotiated by the union, such arbitrary exercise of power by management is much less common. In its place has come the highly legalistic structure of a bureaucracy; and the changing nature of labor-management relations is clearly seen in these two anecdotes told by Jack Bishop.

Don't Fly Too High (Jack Bishop)

A guy, for instance, is restricted from climbing because he's had a little heart problem. And he was not allowed to work because the particular type of work that he done required climbing so he was on medical leave at the time. And while he was on medical leave, he took a physical in order to take pilot's instructions, and he passed the physical to take pilot's instructions, and he was out flying airplanes, and he can't work on his job because he can't climb ladders–the height is supposed to bother him!

Free Vacation with Company Car (Jack Bishop)

And one time a guy came to work, and he apparently had been drinking, and the management thought that he had had too much to drink and that he shouldn't be on the job, and probably rightfully so. If he had been drinking, he might get hurt or hurt someone else. So they was going to send him home for the evening–he was working on the evening shift. And they thought he shouldn't go out in the parking lot and get his car, so the labor relations manager went out and got his car and brought it around to the gate and got out of it and left the brake off and it rolled down into the guardhouse and smashed a fender.

So they had given him a week off, without pay, and then they had to furnish him with a car and take his car and get it fixed because the management had wrecked the fender on his car. So he had a kind of a vacation with a company car, while he was on disciplinary layoff.

Thirty years ago, of course, the worker probably would not have been able to afford an automobile of his own. If he had come to work intoxicated, he would probably have been fired rather than disciplined; and it is highly unlikely that anyone from management would bother to drive his car around for him. The contrast between the management which takes it upon itself to discipline a man for drinking and the management which can commit blunders of this sort provides a wry humor, which probably sums up better than anything else the paradoxical nature of present-day labor-management relations.

Unlike workers in the '30s, workers today have money, and they spend it. When strikes occur, the UAW's strike fund, which usually hovers around $50 million often gets some rather unusual requests for help:

A Long Strike (Jack Bishop)
One particular time, we went on strike, and the committee is always set up before the strike, and they were in operation on the first day, and the guy come in and wanted to know if they could help him out with his electric bill. It was $125. And he had been on strike one day.

While conditions have changed, and workers have less of an emotional attachment for their union, the union still provides a unified front against outsiders and the bureaucracy of the company. In the early days, emotions were strong, and the workers who sided with the company against the union could usually expect trouble. As Clyde Keown said:

During the strike of '37, they had all kinds of trouble. They had one guy, we called him General Motors. Great big man. A guy wanted to hit him, and he took his coat and put it over his head so they couldn't hit him. Then during the strike, a lot of the men was afraid to walk in front of the plant....Some of the guys that didn't agree with us had their ears bashed in.

Today, there is almost no violence of this sort, but the pressure of public opinion, as explained here by Jack Bishop, is equally strong:

There's one thing we do have in our plant. If a guy comes in to work here, of course, in a right-to-work state, he doesn't have to join the union if he doesn't want to. And we've never had this happen. We've had guys not join for about a month, but that's about the extent of it. Usually, the other guys don't use any violence or anything, but if he comes in there and the word gets around that he didn't join or won't join, his treatment is pretty rough, I'd say, because they will work with him–they can't refuse to work with him–but they don't care to. And they don't talk to him, and they don't eat lunch with him or take a break with him. I've never been in that position, but I'd think it would probably give a guy a pretty bad feeling, you know, to be rejected under these conditions.

As opposed to the "scabs" and "finks" who hold out against the union, the workers who belong to the union form a fraternal in-group. Within the union, the terms "brother" and "sister" are common forms of greeting; and while only a handful of members are active in the administrative affairs of the union, a great number campaign actively for one of the top prizes of the year–a trip as delegate to the international convention. Even when times were hard, as related by Clyde Keown, the convention was a big occasion, and members pooled their resources in order to attend.

When they made the first call for our convention, it was in South Bend, Indiana. The guys didn't have no money, and there was no money in the treasury. So one guy rented a room, and I think about eight of them slept in that room. Only had one bed.

Inside the shop, the fraternal feelings manifest themselves in good-natured bantering, such as in the following anecdote:

A Cow and a Calf (Ed Coffey)

One of my best friends on the line: he (laugh) came to work one day with the word that he was going to get married, and it developed that he was marryin' a woman with a child. And I guess to the average individual at times we would probably appear to be most crude and most uncivil and unkind or any other expression you can think of. But you must remember that on the line doing repetitive work, you look for escape. You could either think and do some constructive thought–have some constructive thoughts about what you're going to do when you arrive back home, if you feel like it, or you can tell stories if you get a chance. Or you can pull tricks on people. And when George came in with his word that he was going to get married, we found out who he was going to marry, and then if we wanted to kind of make time pass by making George mad, one of us would say, 'A cow and a calf or a buck and a half,' (laugh) and he would get mad. Oh, he would get mad!

Union Assembly Line Terminology, Slang

The unity provided by the union is perhaps best seen in the terminology or dialect which has developed. In his article on "American Labor Lore" (Industrial Relations, February, 1965, pp. 51-68), Archie Green says that "there is no better way to approach labor lore than by dialect study, for it is a commonplace that groups define and bound their roles by argot and jargon." As Green mentions, labor dialect, rather than defining the ideal labor union member directly, usually consists of pejoratives against those who are not good unionists. While I cannot here go into the detailed study of dialect that Green suggests, my material suggests many of the same conclusions. The terms recalled by my informants–scab, rat, job-killer, carrier, moonlighter, and hillbilly–all reflect on problems created because of fellow workers who did not measure up to the standards of a "good union man."

While "scab" is probably the most widely used labor term, only one of my four informants had any theories about what the word originally meant. Clyde Keown says:

Scab? I don't know, they used to call them scalies and everything else–whether they got the name from a fish but they used to call them scalies and scabs, and they used to call them the foreman's butt boy and things like that.

How he connected scales and scabs is unclear, but the connotation seems closer to the original reference to a skin disease, as explained by Green's article. Whatever the meaning behind the term, none of my informants had any doubt as to the force of the term. Ed Coffey narrated a vivid incident, which was one of the earliest occasions he heard the word used:

In the Ford strike about the same time in Kansas City, I remember, oh, one of the leaders, I can't think of his name, in connection with the battle of Ford Hill–they had the strike breakers come right in through with automobiles. And he walks down the middle of these two lines of automobiles with a baseball bat in his hands and breaking out the windshields of the automobiles. And windows on the sides of both lines as he walked back through there, and they were trying to drive these cars through. But they couldn't get through fast enough to keep him from getting to them with a ball bat, and he broke out a lot of windows in that day and a lot of people were sorry they tried to go through that picket line to go to work. But in that case, there were people standing

In a more enlightened age of labor-management relations, there is little need of the word to describe strike breakers–at least not in such an emotionally charged situation. Yet the word is still in use among younger workers:

Oh, yes, I've heard scab. I don't know, I think if a guy even mentions that it might be good to get back to work or something, he'd be called a scab, you know. You're supposed to be real militant, you know.

And, of course, in states which have "right-to-work" laws, the use of strike breakers is not yet dead, and the term scab often retains all of its former hostility. After a long strike recently at the General Electric plant in Fort Smith, Arkansas, members of UAW Local 716 reacted bitterly against the handful of "scabs" who crossed the picket line. On one occasion, many months after normal operations had resumed, a group of five female employees at the plant followed a co-worker to her home and shouted "scab" at her from their car. When questioned by management about the incident, the women said, "Sure, we called her a scab; that's what she is!" The incident was thought to be of enough significance that the women were all disciplined, and the union's attempts to reverse that discipline were unsuccessful.

The use of the word "rat" is no longer common, but Clyde Keown recalls an incident from the organizing days at St. Louis in which the term was applied in a most vivid manner:

As for dues, as I was telling you, they drew a circle around where a fellow worked, with a rat trap in front of it with a mouse in it. As much as to say he was a rat. They finally got him to come across.

Among the strike breakers in the '30s were the "hillbillies" and "Arkansas travelers"–workers imported in droves from rural areas in the South where wages were low, apparently in an effort to increase competition for jobs and squelch attempts to organize the union. Clyde Keown, who was working in Detroit at this time, explains how the terms were used:

We called 'em hillbillies and Arkansas travelers. A lot of 'em come from Arkansas. And we called 'em Tennessee Hoosiers. A lot of 'em come from Tennessee. Ford ran ads all over the country–this was before they were organized, and they got people from all over the country, and then they turned water hoses on them in below zero weather to keep them away. And here they had advertised for them all over the country.

When not used in a pejorative sense, the term "hillbilly" can also refer to a common phenomenon–the migration to the cities of young rural boys to work in the big automobile factories. This phenomenon is well illustrated by a story which I have hard many times from local union and international staff members about Hiram A. Moon, now Texas Area Director for the UAW:

Catch That Streetcar!

A farm boy from East Texas, Moon came to Dallas to seek a job at the Chevrolet plant. Upon arriving in the city, he asked a passerby how he could get to the plant, and he was told to catch the street car at the next corner. When he was almost to the corner, the street car came whooshing by. Not knowing that there would be more than one street car a day, Moon chased that street car four blocks before he finally caught it! (Retold from memory, learned from UAW associates of Moon in UAW Region 5)

Sometimes, Moon is depicted as being bare footed. At any rate, the picture of the long-legged Texan, who now wears a ten-gallon Western hat and boasts of his personal friendship with President Lyndon Johnson, galloping like a wild horse after the street car provides a comical picture for Moon's associates in the union. It could well be told about a number of former "farm boys."

In many locations today, including the Des Moines plant, a great many farmers work in the plant while hiring out their work on the farm. At a plant in Oklahoma City, these men, who strongly opposed the union, were called "black angus boys." Because they were more interested in job security than in higher wages, they were adamant in their efforts to defeat the union's organizing campaign. In Des Moines, there is no such anti-union attitude among the farmers employed in the plant, but there is some union hostility toward them, as witnessed in the term "moonlighters" which is applied to them. Mike Cole explains:

We had a few of them out there–called them moonlighters. That's a name, they said, 'Well, you're moonlighting there, working the farm.' And, of course, some of those boys tell you, 'Sure, I've got a 300 acre farm down there, and I can hire my help for $1 an hour. I'm a welder here in the plant, so heck, if I can make $3.50 an hour or $4 an hour up here, why it's only costing me $1 an hour for labor to get my work done on the farm.' And, of course, some of the other boys used to rib them and get pretty sarcastic about it...especially if a layoff came, and the fellow that owned the farm had more seniority than the fellow that was getting laid off and maybe the fellow that was getting laid off had a family and here's this guy running the farm and also out there....Some of the fellows would get pretty argumentative. 'Those fellows should be laid off; they shouldn't be allowed to work two jobs.'

One of the most common targets of union rank and filers has traditionally been the International Representative, the person from the international union who helps the local union handle grievances and negotiate contracts. If he tries to supervise their affairs too much, he is, of course, accused to trying to run their affairs. If he lets them take care of themselves, then he is too lazy to give them any service. This animosity toward the International Rep was once manifested in the term "pork chopper," a word which is no longer familiar to younger members such as Jack Bishop. Ed Coffey, one of those at whom the term is aimed, explains it in this way:

They used to call them a very ugly term that we've come away from now, that is about as ugly as many other cliches that we've used in our society–a pork chopper, what we call a pork chopper. Well it means just what it says pretty much. For example, if you're eating regular on the union payroll, you could have those pork chops. Being able to buy meat. You know one of the reasons Miss America is getting bigger every year and why we have so many six foot plus kids in school today, in college, up to seven feet plus, is because, I think CIO wages....They got meat on the table for the first time.

Perhaps the fact that meat on the table is now common among employed workers explains why the use of the word has declined. Certainly, the animosity toward the International Rep is still there, and Clyde Keown is much more frank about it:

Except for a few public relations representatives and actuaries, all of the International Representatives originally worked on the assembly line themselves. Yet their new position with the union makes them white collar workers, and while their pay is not so much higher than many of their co-workers in the shops, they have the enviable position of not having to work on the assembly line; hence, the hostility.

Another traditional practice, which expresses this hostility is explained by Mike Cole. At probably every UAW convention in the last 30 years, and including the 1966 convention, some angry local union delegate has demanded, to no avail, to have all International Reps chased off the convention floor in order to ensure that they do not vote. (International Representatives are forbidden to vote in constitutional conventions. The delegates are concerned that their presence on the convention floor could be used to pad a vote by voice or show of hands.)

Oh, yes, what rank and filers used to call the International Representative has died—used to call them pork choppers. And I've seen conventions, oh boy, they just—some of the

Among other terms used by my informants are "job killer" and "bright haired boy" (already explained above through anecdotes) and "carrier" or "carrier pigeon." The latter, according to Keown, is used to refer to those, usually considered pro-company in the early days, who could always be counted on to pass on the latest bit of gossip or rumor. In the early days, when union members went underground to hold secret meetings, the "carriers" usually took all the proceedings back to the boss. However, Keown says that the boss usually thought more highly of the workers who didn't carry stories than those who did. Keown claims that he and some of his friends used to pass on preposterous rumors to these "carriers"–just to see how far and how fast the story would carry.

Assembly Line Rumors

The "carriers" are apparently still active in the plant since rumors continue to be an important aspect of tradition and custom on the assembly line. They usually reflect the fears, desires, and frustrations of the person on the line. Probably the most prevalent fear concerns job security, and, as a result, the rumors ordinarily involve large layoffs or talk that the plant is closing down or moving to a new location. Many times, of course, they are true; and nothing can be more disruptive than to find that you are suddenly without a job unless you are willing to move to another plant hundreds of miles away. When the Studebaker plant in South Bend, Indiana shut down several years ago, thousands of older workers were left without pension rights for which they had contributed portions of their pay checks for many years. Many former Studebaker employees are still unemployed.

According to Coffey, rumors that the plant is closing down or moving to a new location can be expected to occur during or before contract negotiations. If so, then we can conclude that the "carriers" are still used as convenient tools by management to try to keep workers in a state of insecurity and fear. On the other hand, rumors about layoffs often occur at times when layoffs are most likely. Jack Bishop said, "If they lay off five guys on a Friday, the next Friday there'll be rumors going around that there'll be 120 laid off. Sometimes there's something to it, but most of the time, there isn't." Fortunately, these rumors have tended to disappear with the advent of the guaranteed annual wage negotiated in the 1967 auto and agricultural implement agreements. "A few of the young single guys or some guys that can get along alright on a little less money will be almost happy when they get laid off–for a short while....If he gets sent home, he gets about 50 to 75 percent of his wages for the day anyway....So we don't have much of that rumoring since we have that provision in the contract."

The wishes expressed through rumors do not always have to make sense, however, as seen in the story reported by Ed Coffey:

No More Wheels (Ed Coffey)

Oh, yeah, if the word came out that they were going to be short on wheels or some other part, and we were only going to work until 11 o'clock...that became the longest day. An assembly line is a terrible place for rumors–they just get rumors going on all the time. But the longest day in the week is when the word of a short day comes out, although most of the people on the line would regret losing that much money, income for that day–but to be able to go home is wonderful, and when you don't get to go home, that's the longest damn day you can imagine.

At that time, in the midst of the Great Depression, there was no guaranteed annual wage, and workers desperately needed every piece of employment they could get. The grueling nature of the assembly line becomes even more apparent when we realize that even workers who need money desperately can be disappointed because they are not allowed to go home–without pay.

The rumor reported by Bishop about "plant's growing and they're going to build a new plant" is one that I have not previously heard. Perhaps it is an expression of wish fulfillment for greater job security and maybe even the greater pay and benefits that can be expected to come down from thriving companies.

Slogans

During each convention and each set of national contract negotiations, numerous slogans are circulated to highlight major demands that workers will seek in negotiations: "30 years and out" for a particular pension plan or "parity for aerospace workers" or "$1 an hour now for skilled trades." During the period of negotiations and strikes, these slogans are widely used to unify the membership and provide a focus for their demands. However, most of these slogans are short-range in nature and quickly forgotten once the negotiations are over.

A few, however, especially those culled from speeches by Walter Reuther, president of the international union, still circulate freely. When Reuther demanded job protection for workers who had passed age 45 and hence destined for the industrial job heap, he coined the phrase "too old to work and too young to die." In 1950, when the UAW waged its long strike against Chrysler for a funded pension plan, the phrase became used as a slogan by Chrysler workers all over the country, and it is still frequently mentioned when a union member speaks out for any pension program. The phrase was reported by both Coffey and Cole. A song, written by Joe Glazer and included in the UAW song book and long-play phonograph album, uses this phrase for the title and the refrain.

Songs

Although the international union makes a hearty effort to keep alive the union protest songs of the past, it is doubtful that any of them circulate by word of mouth. Joe Lisi of the UAW Recreation Department travels to union summer schools around the country, playing his guitar and leading group singing of union songs. Hence, graduates of these schools are usually well familiar with "Union Maid," "We're Gonna Roll," "We Shall Not Be Moved," and other union songs. Mike Cole mentions learning "Joe Hill" and "Walter Reuther is our leader" (one verse of "We Shall Not Be Moved"), but he cannot remember the words of any of these songs, and in this he is probably typical of UAW summer school graduates. The old Wobbly song, "Solidarity Forever," is sung at conventions and other union gatherings as the UAW's "national anthem." (It usually takes third billing after "Star Spangled Banner and "Oh, Canada!") Both of the UAW long-play albums, "Songs for a Better Tomorrow" and "This Land Is Your Land," circulate among rank-and-file members and are often played at union meetings or on picket lines.

However, despite all of this exposure, protest songs should probably not be considered an active area of union folklore. Jack Bishop points out that most workers recognize the songs when they hear them and "they know that 'Solidarity' is *our* song," but that is as far as it goes.

When songs are sung, the text followed is nearly always that given in the UAW song book. In this regard, it is interesting to note that both the UAW and AFL-CIO song books retain the revolutionary fourth stanza:

In our hands is placed a power greater than their hoarded gold,
Greater than the might of armies magnified a thousandfold;
We can bring to birth a new world from the ashes of the old,
For the union makes us strong!

Middle class union members blithely sing these words while at the same time they may be harboring their secret fears of the "great liberal/socialist/Communist conspiracy." Yet the more moderate second stanza is omitted from both books:

*It is we who ploughed the prairies, built the cities
where they trade,*
*Dug the mines and built the workshops, endless miles of
railroad laid;*
*Now we stand outcast and starving 'mid the wonders
we have made,*
But the union makes us strong.

Ed Coffey, in a labor education class, once explained this deletion by pointing to the third line of the stanza and then to his rather rounded stomach. "That's the reason," he said. Whether workers feel guilty, as Coffey intimated, about referring to themselves as "starving" or whether they no longer wish to be considered "outcasts," it is definitely true that the stanza no longer has relevance for the American labor movement.

Legends

Changing conditions have also lessened the need for the legends of organized labor. Workers today are more oriented toward the problems of the present and future than the glory of past union battles. Nevertheless, the history of the UAW has been channeled into legends which are usually recognized by most older members and a few historically minded younger ones. "The Battle of the Overpass," where Walter Reuther and other union leaders were severely beaten by company goons during the organization of the Ford Motor Company, is referred to with awe and pride, even though most union members know only a few general details about the event. An aura of myth and legend has also grown up around UAW President Walter Reuther. He still maintains the image of the plucky young fighter, even though he is now in his 60s and keeps a body guard with him at all times. He is known as the clean living Puritan who doesn't smoke or drink and who runs six miles every morning. Yet I recall a union staff member telling a story about Walter's reaction to a grueling negotiation session in the early days of the union. He trudged into the hotel room, grabbed a pint of whiskey, downed what was left of it in one long swallow, and collapsed unconscious on the floor.

Reuther adds to his image as the dedicated hard working union leader by repeatedly refusing to accept wage increases (his salary is now $28,500, extremely low for a man of his responsibility; yet it is definitely not poverty). When the UAW was investigated by the McClellan committee, it was disclosed that Secretary/Treasurer Emil Mazey (whose reputation is even tougher than Reuther's) had once docked Reuther $1.50 on an expense account for a valet charge in a hotel–an item that the frugal UAW refuses to recognize for its staff members. Reuther's body guard once told me that even Walter gets upset when he (the body guard) stops to get a receipt from a cab driver in order to satisfy Mazey's rules for expense statements.

These are all items of the UAW legend, which has been built partially by an adept public relations department, partially by the charismatic qualities of Reuther, and partially by the desire of the membership to look up to a famous leader. Even though many Southern members dislike Reuther's programs on civil rights and progressive legislation, his leadership is not often questioned. A hand shake from Reuther can usually settle a thorny intra-union political problem; a tap of his gavel can quickly quiet a boisterous convention delegation. The explanation can probably be found in these words of Mike Cole:

Walter is a great personal friend of mine. I knew Walter for years. I knew Roy; Roy (Reuther) was another wonderful guy, and I knew them for years, and we've always had our personal arguments....But, by golly, he's a wonderful guy, and I'll support him 100 percent.

...Well, I don't know about his running the six miles, I don't know on that; he might, but I know for a fact he's a good religious man. He doesn't smoke; he doesn't drink; and I know that because I've been very close–I've been in meetings with him and his wife both, just social, where there was something there to drink but Walter never touched it. He'd maybe pick up maybe a bottle of Seven-Up. Because the reason I know that, I don't drink either and between the two of us...

To Mike Cole, Walter Reuther is a famous man, a hero figure; yet at the same time, he is a "personal friend." And this perhaps is the secret behind the UAW legend and most of the rest of the folklore associated with the union. The union is a powerful organization which can take on in battle the fearful dragons–Ford,

General Motors, Chrysler, International Harvester–and win, bringing home wondrous treasures–another 50 cents an hour plus cost of living, improvements in pensions, vacations, and insurance, two additional paid holidays. Yet at the same time, the union is a group of men working together–using stories, jokes, and rumors as a diversion and a protection from the common enemies: the assembly line, the foreman, the time study man, and...boredom.

Conclusion

As it reflects the frustrations, aspirations, and desires of these assembly line workers, the material I have presented above constitutes what I feel is only a small sampling of what could be a vast reservoir of folklore, still untapped in the mass production industries of the United States. While most of the material cited here is presented as incidents that were actually observed and not passed down from past generations of workers (a notable exception is the tale, "Please Save My Plant" on pp. 17-18), they are narrated in much the same way as folk tales. In many cases, I would suspect that certain details are slightly changed or exaggerated to fit the story pattern. I realize, of course, that the four people interviewed are only a small sampling from which no conclusive hypotheses can be drawn. However, I think that the wealth of material which they were willing and anxious to pour out in front of the tape recorder, indicates that there is indeed a great deal of lore in industrial unions just waiting to be gathered by professional folk collectors. Once this collecting is done, I feel confident that many of the stories presented here as eyewitness accounts will prove to be analogues for other stories reported by workers from all sections of the country.

Background Information on Informants

JACK BISHOP–DES MOINES, IOWA

Now 36 years old, Jack Bishop is vice president of UAW Local 991 at Ford Implement in Des Moines and is representative of the younger group of local union leadership. After graduating from high school, Jack joined the Armed Services, spent one year in California working at the massive Convair Aircraft Company, then returned home to work at Ford Implement. From the beginning, he worked on the assembly line and is well familiar with its operation. For the last several years, he has served as vice president of his union and also is a full-time committeeman in the shop–a job in which he deals with the day-to-day problems of workers as well as the negotiating tactics of management. He once served as acting president of his local, when Mike Cole was forced to retire. Bishop now lives with his family, next door to the house in which he was born and raised in Des Moines.

ED COFFEY–ST. LOUIS, MISSOURI

A native of Kansas City, Missouri, Ed Coffey spent most of his teenage years in the Kansas City Boys' Home. Drifting from job to job during the Depression, trying to find steady work, Coffey was once offered a job by the AFL Building Trades–provided he do a little dirty work for them first. A staunch idealist, he refused to take part in violence and hence was not given the job. When he went to work at the Chevrolet plant, he became an early backer of the CIO organizing drive and was a charter member of UAW Local 93. He was soon offered a job on the staff of the international union, and he served as political action and educational representative for the UAW in Kansas City, St. Louis, and Dallas before being appointed Assistant Director of Education for the international union in Detroit. He is now Education Director for Region 5 UAW and organizes summer schools, conferences, and seminars for union members in eight middle and southwestern states–Missouri, Arkansas, Louisiana, Oklahoma,

Texas, Colorado, and New Mexico. Now 64 years old, Coffey has continued to maintain close contact with assembly line workers from nearly every part of the country.

MIKE COLE–DES MOINES, IOWA

Born 40 miles west of St. Joseph, Missouri in 1904, Mike Cole moved with his family to Centerville, Iowa in 1913. Mike's father was a railroader, and young Mike got his first taste of union life when he joined his father on the picket line during the railroad strike of the 1920s. "My father was a strong union man," he said. "He stood about 6 foot 1 or 2 and weighed about 200 pounds. He could just bend over and pick up a 300-pound railroad rail just like it was nothing. And I seen him take two guys–scabs as they called them–that was trying to cross the picket line–just take two of them and crack their heads together and throw one in each direction." The railroad brought in strike breakers from the South, and the union lost the strike, but Mike's father refused to go back to work for the railroad. After graduating from high school, Mike moved to Rockford, Illinois, where he worked for Roper Stove Company, but when the Depression hit, he was forced to return to Centerville to work on the farm until the Depression was over. After three years as owner of a small coal mine (see story, pp. 18-19), Mike moved to Des Moines and went to work at what was then Wood Brothers Implement Company and now Ford Implement. Mike started work at the plant in 1944–three years after it was organized by the UAW. "The plant was originally organized in 1936 under the old F-E local, the old farm implement union," Mike said. The workers voted decertification and went UAW in 1941 because "we thought UAW was a better international, and, at that time, the F-E was pretty well dominated by Communists." Before being forced to retire in June, 1964, Mike Cole spent nearly all of his working career as an officer of his union. Six months after he started work, he was elected steward, then served on the bargaining committee, and for the final 18 years of his working life, he served as president of UAW Local 991, an exceptionally long reign for the highly political office of local union president. He now lives with his daughter and grandchildren only a few blocks from the plant and union hall and is still often counted on for help and advice.

CLYDE KEOWN–ST. LOUIS, MISSOURI

Born on a farm near Alhambra, Illinois (located about 20 miles east of St. Louis), Clyde Keown moved with his family to Granite City in 1910. His ancestors, Scotch-Irish immigrants, had moved to Illinois many years earlier through Kentucky and the Carolinas. From 1915 to 1930, Keown worked for General Motors in Detroit where he observed first-hand the conditions which lead to unionization of the auto industry. Back at the Fisher Body plant in St. Louis, Clyde was a participant in early organizing efforts of the UAW and was inside during the sit-down strike of 1937. A charter member of one of the largest UAW locals in the Midwest, Local 25, Keown held several offices in his local union. Now 77, he is president of the St. Louis Area UAW Retirees Club and an active worker for the United Fund and other community service projects.

Index to Folklore Materials

TALES, ANECDOTES

Heroes, Fast Workers

Tragic Cases

Just a Little Relief

Bosses, Foremen, and Efficiency Experts

Strikes, Discipline Cases

Humor

CUSTOMS, RITUALS

TERMINOLOGY

RUMORS

SLOGANS

9 781720 360681